C000138912

THE DRAFT WILL

PETER ROBINSON

THE DRAFT WILL

for Paula & Jonathan
warm regards,
Peter
17 Sept 2015

ISOBAR
PRESS

Published in 2015 by

Isobar Press
Sakura 2-21-23-202
Setagaya-ku
Tokyo 156-0053
Japan

http://isobarpress.com

ISBN 978-4-907359-11-9

Copyright © Peter Robinson 2015
All rights reserved.

ACKNOWLEDGEMENTS

Earlier versions of 'The Draft Will' and fourteen of the prose poems in the opening section appeared in *Untitled Deeds* (2004). 'The Fog' was first published in *Ghost Characters* (2006). I am grateful to Chris and Jen Hamilton-Emery for publishing the former volume, and John Lucas for the latter. 'Liverpool … of all places' was written as a prose contribution to the anthology *Liverpool Accents: Seven Poets and a City* (1996). 'Hit the Road, Jack' was composed for the centenary of Linacre Infants and Junior School, but not published. 'Becoming a Reader' was commissioned by *The Reader* and appeared in their issue 13 (2003). 'A Performing Art' was requested for *The Cambridge Review* 106, no. 2287 (1985) and published to coincide with the Poetry Festival of that year. 'In a Tight Corner' first appeared in *News for the Ear: A Homage to Roy Fisher* (2000). Sir Hugh Cortazzi commissioned 'Lost and Found' for *Japan Experiences: Fifty Years, One Hundred Views* (2001). 'Behind "Otterspool Prom"' was written for *The Reader*'s 'Poets at Work' series and appeared in issue 36 (2009). My thanks go to the editors of these various publications.

Contents

For Ornella, Matilde and Giulia

SIDE EFFECTS

Not much of the room remains. Just two walls meet at a cornice with some peeling paper and raw brick, its stepped edge hard against sky. Still, we've a doorframe, the door ajar, a few sticks of furniture on a red rug, the pine board floor; and, beyond this open-air interior, a brown-tinged hillside with greenish distance fading as far as the mountains. Here at a table, here's English herself sat on the single cane chair. Her hair in a chignon, she's wearing a chic evening gown like a hospital robe, one tender breast exposed. She's whispering phrases in my good ear.

I'm half stood up as if to leave. A splayed hand palm-down on the table, waistcoat a bit the worse for wear, yet still I'm here – and, true, where else would I go from this neither in nor out? Dark clouds flare, gilt-edging the horizon. What am I saying? Wide eye appealing to the woman in white, lips parted, with an amorous look.... Distinctly mixed prospects fleck the sky. Is it anything to do with promises un-kept? Ineptitude? Scandal? Resentments only? Or debts nobody should be asked to pay?

'You've taken the words right out of my mouth,' she says, putting words into mine.

A Woman a Poem a Picture

for David Inshaw

The flattened cumulus darker than slate allows bright sunshine to break across the gap between cloud-banks and the tumuli as, elsewhere, topiary hedges. Would it be a woman reaches up to readjust her – what's it called? – a parasol. Or, no, she waves goodbye.

Dilapidated circumstances: lacking its flimsy white covering, Thomas Hardy ('greatest of the moderns') imagined the one he had come across a skeleton. Well, he would.

The deepening presence of … what if she leaves him? Clouds are heaped. A mackerel sky has evening written all over it. Not very much gets finished. Now you count two women, together, playing shuttlecock. Best to keep it under your hat was William Blake's advice, for love that's told can never be.

And she has turned face into the sun. The yellow verso of her breasts diminishing, this shadow may well be extended – and to whatsoever distance. Embed small dabs of darker tone in the field behind her.

It's difficult to draw with the woman in his light. The painter's set up his easel in that green, but his model refuses, point-blank, to stand still.

At the Invitation View, it remains unclear who has returned and from what oblique, unwished-for angle. The colour match depends on whatever she is wearing: no, hardly the original air-blue gown. It's the unexpected appearance of another person's wife, who stops herself from smiling and goes on up the stairs.

If I Hold the Words

When I hold the words in focus, she's soft colour-fringe against white margins, and merges into forgotten textures of chair and wall – photography.

The street turns away from my page's edges, but it can't be helped. Where cars pause at the lane-end, she smiles, and at a corner disappears.

His articulated trailer twists; the driver, demolishing our lamppost opposite … night darkens.

Imagine it occurring to me then. At concealed entrances, the trunk road, like memory, promises returns.

You reappear at half-past-nine.

As if I'd had it planned.

The Fog

Her father's death would mean the end. The dustsheets are thrown on in Via Bixio. Ghosts of chairs and tables freeze among air-roots of plants, heavy rustic sideboards, marble floors, her old prints of the city, and a swirling abstract picture. But now I've to leave them in his poor corner, hunched up on the bed perhaps, around them typescripts, scrawls, turned pages, chess men, dictionaries, and the fierce cold. They'll be talking quietly. Her whole world – it had seemed so much more secure than his – was suddenly falling in pieces. Her father, by means of a promissory note, had sunk the family fortune in another's bankruptcy. A lifelong friend had been his ruin.

So what was this friend of mine trying to achieve? He would help her through the perishing season, would help her over an unspoken wound. Yet at the funeral, he'd been called an inter-loper. They would accuse him of only wanting her money, her inheritance. Inheritance? The family was putting what property remained into different names, to save the little left, though even the lawyers – as it transpired – were picking clean their bones.

Now I'm in that icy damp, nose streaming on the Ponte Catena. The fog's so dense both San Zeno and Borgo Trento have com-pletely disappeared. There's just this greyness everywhere, a blurry orange glow before me – Renon's ice cream parlour – the only kind of reassurance…. Her people are like frozen statues in that park back there: the relations between them obscure, the dramatis personae a muddle of names. Yet dear among them is his blonde Italian, with a butterfly grip in her drawn-back hair. She'll be sat beside him on that rumpled bed. He'll have his arm around her shoulder. He's trying to talk himself back into her life.

14

In Venice Once

for Isabel Via Vera

In Venice once, a door was opened. From that place of carnival masks, of gondolas, accordions' arpeggios squeezed down back canals, you showed a way past sodden palazzi resolutely wrapped in restorers' gear, from the absolute cliché of Saint Mark's fed pigeons, the Japanese honeymoon souvenirs, daubed oil-on-canvas views of a Venice where everything seemed for sale.... You showed a way to the cool hotel room where our girls could play.

In Venice, once, a passageway opened on a silent playground surrounded by plane trees, classroom windows, and a hollow bell tower. There, we met the school's custodian, a survivor of the city's fame, who fed us pasta, peas, and wine on her rooftop terrace. This too was an island of lucky neglect no distance from the dead-end alleys, fetid waters, and traipsings through that swarming place.

One yellow plane leaf had touched down like a waiter hovering by my plate. And how could I not recall our would-be therapeutic days? We were seeing if its marble might make us some amends.

In Venice once when a door was opened, we tried, we tried God knows. But it would be others who gave us back ourselves.

In the half-sleep of our wagon-lit there were the usual trundling sounds, a clatter of points, uncoupling engines; but then I could sense we'd been stopped a long while, as at a halt or station, where passports would be checked – and our night train was anyway ringed with voices. But the views from that compartment hardly recalled banlieux of Paris. It was more like a postcard with Lago Maggiore, an island village campanile, a ferryboat passing between it and us.... It was true: we were stopped outside Baveno, our last coach derailed by a signalman switching his points too soon. We were stopped for hours not far from Stresa one fine March morning, hungrily alive. No, it wasn't the fact that I'd slept through the crash ... but being so thrown back with its faint jolt, back down the years of waking dreams, of mistakes and damage, I was reminded how hard it can be, how hard just to cross a frontier.

Two Lost Houses

1

It would make me think of our lost houses.... Yes, we'd go back a long way if – beyond the cloistral vegetation, daffodils, crocuses, the tree-lined avenues and gates' wrought-iron, the railings behind real tennis courts – you trespassed with me on the gravel drive of 5b Herschel Road. Instead, I'm alone at this promised sticky-end, reading a notice of planning permission: the house being broken into flats, work on the project already begun. I can see the stripped walls, smashed tiles, bare wires, and a filled skip parked outside. Now, nose pressed to the murky glass, I'm staring back through empty rooms, taking in dilapidations, sorry attempts to make repairs – like fragments of the things you said, or a skylight flared with stars.

2

It's like in some bad dream. He pulls a snapshot from his pocket to show the house up on its hillside, with roofs and campanile behind, a house overgrown; and I know, can imagine the bramble-choked path as he talks, the threshing floor waist-high in weeds, can imagine the neighbour as she says, 'Yes, bought years ago by an English couple, an English couple not seen here again....' It's like in some bad dream; and as he goes on about the earthquake-damaged house, each rain-soaked, staved-in beam, each collapsed or collapsing floor, its façade just a door that swings onto nothing, I mean to mention the deadlocked deeds, that there's no such thing as a no fault divorce.... But I don't say a word.

THE PAVILION

Why can't you leave it alone in its grounds, that red-brick pavilion in dusk light, late June, with an aura of linseed, smeared grass juice, worn kit – why can't you leave it alone?

Under the hoarding by a footbridge over branch lines, my bare legs burned with raised stings from the nettles' many-pointed leaves, and I learned to recognize clumps of dock by their rusty shapes. Like the family's generations of women who would gather herbs and balms, I learned the remedies' self-healing terms.

Now even the thought of it does me some good – as if each question had a response, each pain came with its cure. Deep in the dumps or in pieces, I think of how they picked those leaves to rub on tender places, how they found common aids for every sore.

'A nettled egalitarian' were the words he used. That's how the phrase ran, and saw right through me. But what had happened to that idea, to the nettled egalitarian needing dock-leaves aplenty to ease his doubled sting?

At dusk on one of those late June days, with an outfield stretching before us, I saw the pavilion, its green gables, white-faced clock, and red-brick warm in the sun's long fade. Beyond the boundary fence, not much after close of play and its disappointments, among dandelions and railings, there were the rust-edged clutches of dock; and there beyond that boundary fence, it seemed best to be up and gone.

Still I'm haunted by things I didn't do, like having my collar felt as in a dream some nights ago. Come up at traffic lights, he proceeded to book us, and I got the policeman's suspicious peering look, his 'Didn't you used to live here once?'

Then that pavilion's an emblem of exams I failed to reach in time, or somehow never did quite pass in nightmares woken from again on summer dawns like this.

THE ESCORTS

Quiet on the pleasure craft, they're staring at sunset's cloud convoys, at strata, heads of hair, each clustered wind-blown pine. Some of the islands have fishing smacks, wharves hung with tyres, blue-roofed sheds and telephone poles. The waves are staked for seaweed farms, or oyster beds, crab traps marked by fluttering flags on their bamboo spears, frayed in a breeze.

The escort seabirds, attentive off our wake, with eyes right, dive to catch in avid mouths, whether gull or tern, the food scraps hurled at them. We're watching those creatures zigzag, balanced on currents of air, then drop to bob and gulp down bits of nourishment there in the widening foam. Sometimes they swoop so close you can almost touch their yellow beaks.

Perhaps that voice, as it laced each phrase with apologetic sighs, with thanks for being allowed to exist, being almost out of earshot in rejuvenating wind, inspired him to throw his bearded head back, extend an arm round her slender neck, to grasp at one last happiness no matter what the cost in chaos, the allies tried and friends offended.

Embracing there, they gazed across that planking deck at every wave-carved, pine-topped island.

Matsushima

'She's ugly, though,' that man had said, as he turned away from a girl in profile, one playing her theorbo by Gerard Terborch. His lady companion had seemed to agree as they sidled along to its neighbour. Beside them, I couldn't help but smile.

The young Dutch girl with a kind of lute was plucking her tune – an accompaniment for the two gallants leaning at a still-life table. Its gallery caption would have us decide: was it a brothel, or domestic scene?

One of those fellows, absorbed in the music, appears to vocalize his score. A cat toys with something caught up in her skirts. An ace of clubs, slipped to the floorboards, doesn't leave much room for doubt. With the carved sound-hole and its swollen bowl, even her fingered theorbo was doubtless a punning innuendo.

The painter has finely glazed her fur-trimmed, satin gown. But that weak profile and recessive chin, what were they meant to express? I was staring at her smile-less face, a mirror to nature, need and loss, but not, it appeared, at someone debauched … and neither at her ugliness.

Personal Boxes

'en el interior de tus cajas
mis palabras se volvieron visibles'
Octavio Paz

1

Boxed in by schoolgirls on a tram, its separate compartments crammed full of faces, identical sailor-suit uniforms, small voices like disappearing mosquitoes at home time ... that's how to head for a Cornell exhibition beyond the eastern mountains.

2

Or, by contrast, changing trains, we're stood on a near-empty platform, all but seeing the words reach inches from our mouths, then echo as if off the glass cases which seem to enclose us – English words gone unrecognized by the ginkgo and bamboo in late autumn.

3

Leaves rain down on this bright day, a November, in the Culture Zone. You shuffle past exhibits reflected in swathes of maple and oak across each windowpane. You hear a far-off accordion from the landscaped garden where parents' backs are stuck with leaves tossed over them by joking kids still tumbled in the autumn's lap.

4

And even if sights of a gibbous moon rising in the still light sky or leaf-smoke plumes through a stand of pine bring back uncalled-for memories, surely you might have known?

5

All those constructions of Joseph Cornell's couldn't but remind us of the hotel rooms in Tokyo. Tempted by soft porn on the box, or a fridge that bills for a peek inside, I'd be sick of the hum from a fixed air-con with misted-over, sealed-up windows – epitome, if ever there was one, of being no more than alive, alone, and left to your own devices.

6

'There are things you can't come back from,' this friend of mine let slip. We were waiting in a glass-walled bus stop, 'like words you wouldn't want to fault, yet still they're screening off your past.'

7

But then leaves gusting over asphalt in their autumn tones replied, 'Oh, don't take life too personally.'

Shiga

SIDE EFFECTS

When death cuffed me across the face, I didn't turn the other cheek, but flinched, and from one corner of an eye, the wide right-field blur shaded into night.

Now mountains come at me askance. Along a road home's snaking curves, earth's rim, its margin, is hazed in dusk. Sun flares through cloud-wisps trailed above the tree fringe, frayed, and now in silhouette.

I keep an eye on it, blood streaming in the firmament. Broadcasting tower and a Ferris wheel glint at that distance. Though it's almost five o'clock, the light of day still lingers. I keep an eye on it, twisting my neck that bit more to the right.

It's like wiping the smile off one side of your face. Now that slice of death still stares me down from any bathroom mirror. There a temple and part-unlined forehead don't live up to who they are – as if I had no strains or stresses, time couldn't leave its mark on me, as if a half a life weren't over.

Sendai

Fairground Dusk

1

Skirting the fairground's painted forms, as if inside a kaleidoscope,
I gaze through the strut-work of Corkscrew and Pirate. Beyond
all this semi-transparency, offering little resistance, neon flickers
across a gorge; the late sun flashes round shadows of branches –
like interior detail or a colour slide.

2

But stopped by the lights at our Luna-Park, what it is about that
full moon above the Big Dipper I can't put my finger on? The
carousel, dodgems and swing-boats make it feel like ... I can't
find it in me to say, though it's there on the tip of my tongue.

Summer Cinema

1

This morning's lizard scoots across a cracked half-brick, its home.
The ants have made an early start on crumbs from last night's
table. Unreachable spiders spin behind grey radiators.

Yellow flowers of the broom are splashed above a window
frame. A half-drunk bottle's once-frothy wine is still where we
left it, open all night, in a *nature morte* with pans and dishes, the
washing-up still to be done

But let them rest a moment longer day-dreaming in the calm
of their position, as early sunlight picks at leftovers or grants to
crumbs a measure of shadow, and to each its own.

2

Rising towards a hole in the eaves, white pigeons with splayed
tails are ruffling the undergrowth. Wasps panic and take to the
air, fleeing their home – a spray-attacked crack in warped, paint-
spattered grain.

Despite precautions, the telltale hum of mosquitoes rises and
fades near family members dozing under roof-beams.

Silhouetted against the sun-flare, in a cloudless dusk's pink
glow, on harvested earth ploughed over, the well-fed guests
spread out across spaces framed by a kitchen door.

They are all gone into the light – or that's how it seems from
inside, this interior dark for whoever's left holding the baby.

3

Cracks in the plaster show structural damage, acute-angled shadows under doors. In a breeze, great tendrils flail; the hammock weave's frayed with the years.

Under a pergola's trailing vines, political discussions unravel their threads. The day grows dark, more substance in the shadows cast than in their still-life objects.

Earlier memories return at wrong times: like daylight moons in a plainer air, but whatever do they come back for?

See the caught flies languish on spiders' webs, on sticky strips, or on each baffling glass pane.

The picture windows' multi-screens form an amphitheatre for the cloud heaps, sun-scapes, the morning mist.

Tinged surfaces, mute survivals – flaked stucco speaks volumes to those adept at reading walls.

4

The projector's lodged on a terrace beam beneath the full moon's even light, a film continuing out of doors.

The story's set in a place like this with isolate houses on a ridgeway two fields wide, all exposed to the elements, to wind-gusts bringing changes, seasonal changes and the others.

After midnight, the summer cinema's still being shown on a whitewashed wall with falling stars above and, falling asleep below, assembled neighbours in repose. Among farm implements and toys, they're slipping away from the grip of fiction.

Then the titles roll, the soundtrack fades – as if the thing were reluctant to leave us, and leave not a trace of how we lived behind.

ZONA DI RISPETTO

1

Leaf carpets on a patio give way to sun-struck hillside cut across,
striated by long morning shadow. Last fruits of the year are clinging
to a persimmon the blackbirds' beaks and low sun light upon.

2

A girl's face framed by furniture, a pale Madonna in its niche,
the wayside shrine, her future's locked there, caught through
time, behind a black wrought iron gate, glimpsed as we pass by
in our careering car....

3

Lizards scoot across the pink scratched plaster of a garage wall.
Dust plumes, a dog's persistent howl rise behind car tyres. Russet
leaves and tabloid pages tell of weekend bloodbaths. Invisibly
scarred by near deaths, it's miraculous youth heals.

4

A pomegranate's bitter juice and brusque wine banish glints of
candelabra on deep-shaded mirrors. Those juices enter other
alcoves, another time, light bringing back our happiness once
more to this countryside. A pair of doves pause on a pole with
sun-struck hillsides, other loves. Yet they're as sudden gone.

5

No doubt, but then again, above these cities of the plain a low sun
lights on sodden greens, on browns – autumnal duties laid aside
a moment in the milder distance, if you see my point of view.

Parma

Behind a small gasworks long since closed, we stop at the traffic lights almost every day. There's a thousand Lire note on the dash in case your friend comes emerging from between sparse shrubs at the foot of an embankment, detergent bottle and cloth in hand.

With him, you always nod agreement, offer the note before he's sprayed or swabbed the screen. So, if hours later, we pause at the lights once more, he doesn't ask, but waves and smiles and passes to the next car.

Romanians, or so you tell me, dreamed up this job-creation scheme, as I glance along the gasworks wall with its pasted layers of posters for the *Festa del unità* in villages around.

And before the lights change, I'm already wondering what brought him here – escaping what humiliation, across what frontier, track or choppy strait, to find life in this wealthy town.

But now, where his things were, the ground's quite bare; and in this August heat, he's gone. Perhaps the Council's cleared them from the streets, or your friend has lost his obscure protection.

Whatever, I nearly see him. With his finger-less gloves in a winter's chill, with just so much time, he races down the exhaust-fume defile of engines ticking between wall and embankment.

Across the great gulf of each windscreen, in wide sweeps his quick hand moves, revealing through the foamy glass impassive fellow Europeans – darkly, and then face to face.

THE BLUE SHELTERS

for Alastair Morgan

For a breath of air we're following the thread of a route you take
through cherry trees in winter; there's nothing else for it, and out
we have to go. Along raised walkways among enormous spaces,
their vastnesses absorbing us, we've seen as much as anyone,
needing a breath of air.

Flanked by towering blocks and the gulfs of a rail embankment,
by the labyrinthine alleyways, drained moats and broad canals,
we're streaked with networks of interlaced branches. All around,
illumination blinking in the twilight, we see through expanses
of accumulated plate-glass, through unlit fronts, their windows
reflective of yet more night.

And there's this thread of talk between us, multiplied reflections
we followed past blue sheet-shelters built upon park benches.
The time's late for their occupants; they have slipped through
other networks to a walkway's prospects of the capital with
gnarled cherry trees in winter. Here, last possessions are neatly
in their places. No resentment, or so it seems, the remnants of
their self-esteem lie here in these blue shacks.

There's nothing else for it; in our talk are stock-and-share-war
rumours murmured round old Edo; nothing else for it with
temperatures dropping, snow forecast for the small hours – and
nobody needing to get out more.

POETIC JUSTICE

I

Crows fly among the moonlit pines, return to their nests in threes or fours as I climb past outworks of the castle walls. Street lamps are shiny in branches, bark's silvered, everything astir on the walk back home. Tired, I'm making my way towards someone who no longer needs this: for she has her man – and the one who won you with words, he senses flakes soften on eyelids, thinks himself gone and forgotten –

2

but wrongly. Worn down by the children, somehow you resist till dark; and now as the grip of obligation tightens, still I'm reading ice patches of un-trodden drift, slant glimpses of a half-moon through branches, and thinking how you were my love … mistakenly. You are. Then, jacket flecked with snowmelt, I've returned and closed the door. But well you know how I thrive on neglect. You get more out of me that way.

Sendai

THE PAST

i.m. Fumiko Horikawa

It was already dusk when we walked into the hills and, looking back, could pick out, among darker profiles, the places we had been. Down there, from the scrum of a shoe-removing room to a quiet, raked stone garden with its adventitious wall was but a few shuffled paces. Was it emptiness or central calm? No, they were simply rocks and gravel. Whatever, it wasn't the same, this interplay of stain and edge, as five crammed years before. Arranged, those grey things there, I hadn't had the heart to see.

'The past is past,' that's what he said. We were haunting the sacred wood shrine.

He said it at the memories mentioned, as if the past were like our shoes. But they couldn't be undone, their scents just yards away in my one-time home with ghost-lives beyond a clump of pines. It was there in the moss-encrusted thatch, a weathered wood stage for fertility rites, for dances, in a sunset's last gleam where we watched, in autumn leaves and temples, fitting like a foil for fresh signs of fulfillments you'd not survive to live, while we had got this far.

Kyoto

Domestic Epigrams

1

Past the ranks of trees, a thicker darkness than tonight's, come glinting flashes in windows, cars negotiating back streets, or street lamps themselves; and as I move they blur, bleed into one another, like blasts seen through tears from further wars, signals in blockaded gulfs, or black-out violations. Still, here, our children are snoring, and the flat is calm.

2

And there in the small hours, with screens, tatami, futons full of dreaming family, a cloud of vapour fills the room. A humidifier, set too high, has been left on to pump out gouts of white steam.

3

I come back to the door and find a cloud-sea's snowy mountains, islands rising from the foam, or a nipple hill at dawn with plumed evaporating rains – not a dry eye in the house. So much of life's set on keeping wetness in its place, but celebrate it, let it thrive. And come back to the door past midnight, it's into that whiteness I climb.

Year-Forgetting

Out of sight, round further curves, the traffic murmurs on high bridges. Two women tend allotments above the neap-tide line.

The stream here's wide enough for skipping stones. They make five bounces off its surface, but, short of the far bank, sink.

The cliff's rock strata are stacked so we see sandstone, humus, and the topsoil. Houses and flats are crowded at its edge. It's just a few days before New Year.

But seeing as how a home's foundations can open up beneath our feet to fold the floor-tiles like a blanket, don't ask where the old year went, or care to have one thought too many.

Follow the river round past these allotments, carry on left or right, go back.

For in this surviving meander, it's as sure as what remains of the short day's light.

There's no crossing over here.

The Draft Will

THE DRAFT WILL

1

After a maze of brick terraces, among corner shops and pubs, beyond a garage with its Michelin Man's body of swollen white tyres, the house stood at a row-end, abutting on an abattoir.

It stood behind its own low wall, where the rusty stumps of railings taken for the war effort stood out from its capstones.

Over the wall, some rough grass, weeds and brambles thrived in a patch of front garden.

The front door's layers of paint were cracked apart to form islands like a mud flat in dry weather.

2

A white plate on that cracked black paint showed the house number, above it an oval, frosted glass pane.

Now grandma comes to darken this oval. She opens the front door, stoops for a kiss on her loose-skinned face, and welcomes us down a corridor leading past a sitting room we aren't supposed to enter.

It's furnished with stiffly sprung, coarse-covered chairs. There are sideboards, and pot plants in bowls on the what-nots.

Crowding a chest of drawers, her family photos rest in their beaten metal frames: uncle Bobby in the Home Guard, granddad on a steamship's deck, dad in an Anglican choir boy's robes....

The parlour where grandma spent her days felt spacious in the eyes of a child. On the left was another large chest, its drawers filled with letters, bits of string, odds and ends like call-up papers, an identity tag from the war.

Above it there hung a huge monochrome photo of dad – aged two or three years old – in polished black boots and a white cotton dress.

His face is thin with small mouth and deep-set eyes. The eyes are so sunk in their sockets they look cast in shadow – as if he's not been sleeping well, has been in a fight, or suffers from some wasting illness.

He was treated as a delicate boy through childhood, though blessed all his life with good health.

4

On shelves in the corner stands a Negro minstrel moneybox. There's a slot in one hand so the singer can raise and swallow small coins. But how could you ever get them out once they were in?

'You can't,' mum said.

When we took him down and shook him, no coins rattled in his red-costumed chest.

5

Grandma's room was focused by a black range-fire. Perhaps before the war she still used it for cooking.

There's a polished copper kettle, smoke-darkened on the side turned away from the family. Now a small cast-iron gas stove has been moved into her scullery.

One afternoon, as we sat by that kettle, dad drew two family trees. They showed three generations, from the grandparents down to us boys.

By the bus stop, when we set off home, some fiercely pollarded stumps loom behind air-gnawed iron railings. From those massive tree trunks, tenuous branches have started to shoot – like arrows from an Indian's quiver.

6

Hanging on the wall is a painting of a ship in a storm. The ss *Hardanger* has a tall narrow funnel, hardly any cabins or bridge for superstructure, two masts, and a black hull with red band near the waves.

Nor has the painter missed its plimsole line beside the bows. The sea is flecked with foam, the sky a mass of billowy grey. The ship pitches at an angle, stern up as it battles through high seas.

The dining table, only moved out at mealtimes, was usually pushed below that ship-on-the-wall's wood frame. You could stand on the table to get a closer look – if you promised not to touch the thick paper.

Edging across its white cloth, catching a glimpse of the family far below, you knew the anaglypta would give to your touch. It made a faint rustling sound, then plaster dust sifted through onto the floor.

Yes, it seemed as if the wallpaper were holding up the wall.

That steamship was a relic of granddad's travels, but nobody could remember from where he'd brought it back.

A cardboard box of black-and-white postcards showed places granddad said he'd been. Some of them were joined together. They cascaded to the lino like a postcard concertina: views of Valparaiso, Chicago, Timbuctoo....

His gaze ever fixed on those farther shores, my granddad went out to Canada. He would bring the others over later.... Or perhaps just leave them back in Manchester.

But come home to emigrate with the family, he'd applied for nationality – only to be turned down on account of his poor health.

Grandad was a dreamer, so the story went, his hopes of escape or a fresh start over there getting no further than that job as a restaurant-car waiter (or so he said) on the Canadian Pacific Railway.

Lunch finished, we'd be sent out to play. That way, they could have some peace and quiet. Beyond the scullery, a yard with its ramshackle shelves was where grandma kept her tub and dolly posser. There were blocks of hard white chalk among the clutter. Mum took a piece and scratched step-numbers on the flags. Hopscotch would keep us busy for a while.

Then there was the wilderness of garden to explore: granddad's vegetable patch grown over, the contraptions of wire mesh and wood once his hen coops now fallen in disrepair. Farther, we could venture across the sunken flags and flooding grids of an alley down Claremont Road.

Up the stairs, at the bedroom door, one time we glimpsed the place where uncle Bobby's teeth were pulled. The gas canister had been dragged all the way up those stairs.

Dad suffered from boils on his neck caused by the Thirties diet, so grandma sewed his collars a size too large for when he went to school.

Why did uncle George die before our dad was born? Grandma molly-coddled our dad. No, she hadn't spoiled him – how could they afford that – but half stifled him in anxious cotton wool.

They got by on granddad's vegetables, his eggs, an occasional hen – her neck wrung the first time she laid one that smelt bad. There's a picture of granddad wearing a trilby hat, holding in his arms a large white bird. Yes, he even won prizes for his poultry.

Why did this penurious, frequently unemployed man always vote Conservative? How could granddad – who supplemented what income he earned by growing greens and keeping hens – have made out he was a propertied man? Trying to seem dignified in his own wife's eyes? What had their childhoods been? No, there were no memories, nothing. Our history was a blank.

In old age granddad sat tapping his fingers on the arm of his chair, tapping his fingers from boredom, from boredom, bored with himself, with his life.

In that final illness he was taken into hospital, and suddenly it was over. He died because he'd given up. He had had enough. That was our first death, the first known face to disappear forever, with its angular features, the hollow eye sockets, and a thin grey widow's peak. It was in those sockets his dream of life had curdled, punished in and by the great pretend of his own life, a life that had passed on, that had been passed on, woven from bits of story and from silence.

But it turned out mum thought she'd known all along. Her mother-in-law was a chatterbox, mum nothing if not a great listener well able to keep her own counsel.

Did dad know his wife was onto granddad's secret? It shouldn't have come as any great surprise that he had one – what with all the stories he would tell, the might-have-beens and wishful thinking.

Now what mum was saying as we stood at the sink one summer morning was that dad's father had been born to his dad's fancy woman.

And did dad know granddad's secret too? Yes, he'd come across a paper among the heaps gone through when grandma could no longer look after herself. She had come to live with us, her home's contents sold to a house-clearing firm.

That's what became of the ss *Hardanger*. No one thought to keep it, and, never one to wax nostalgic, dad had wanted shut of the lot. The place was left derelict; but one day driving past, he'd glanced round and saw the yellow lace curtains still flapping at its broken panes.

Grandma never threw anything away. Her cupboards overflowed with bits-and-bobs, threads of cotton, wartime airgraphs, letters, snaps, and such like. There, dad had found this document, made of cartridge paper, and composed in a flowing, official-looking hand.

The back, when the document was folded, formed a cover. On it had been written: 'Dated 11th [*deleted*] 12th day of August 1891 / Draft / Will of Thomas / Fisher / Robinson'. 'Draft' looked inserted as if an afterthought. The word was on a line of its own, squeezed in between the date and the title.

'This is the last will and testament of me Thomas Fisher Robinson of 26 Ross Street off Hyde Road Ardwick Manchester in the County of Lancaster Commission Agent. I hereby revoke all wills and testamentary dispositions heretofore made by me and declare this my only will made and executed the twelfth day of August one thousand, eight hundred and ninety one. I devise all my real estate (if any) and I bequeath all my personal estate unto and to the use of my natural son James [Fredrick] Robinson (whose mother was Elizabeth Hewitt) absolutely and I appoint my said son James [Fredrick] Robinson aforesaid and my friend James Broome of Brook Street Manchester aforesaid Beer Retailer Executors of this my will. [The day and year first before witness] In witness whereof I have hereto set my hand. Signed by the testator Thomas Fisher Robinson as and for his last will and testament in the presence of us present at the same time, who at his request, in his presence, and in the presences of each other have hereunto subscribed our names as witnesses....'

From this long-hoarded paper dad knew for sure he'd been named after his grandfather. He believed the parts in pencil – like his dad's middle name, and the various corrections – would make the will invalid, since they hadn't been initialed. In spite of this, it looked as if great-granddad thought the will was good, for it was both signed and witnessed.

Looking more closely, though, clearly the names of the witnesses were written in the same hand as the document and signature. Wouldn't the witnesses have had to sign the will?

How odd that granddad had been made an executor: he was only ten in 1891. Perhaps the will's being so vaguely worded was reason enough for it to be ignored, for it never to have been acted upon?

The testator had written it in his best penmanship. He had signed it with his more relaxed hand. Then he had taken advice on its validity – only to be told that he needed to give the full name of his natural and only son (he had at least three daughters), and that the declaration by the witnesses had also to include the date.

Discovering it wasn't valid he had added the word 'Draft'. Perhaps he intended to make a proper version, but nothing of the like was ever found.

Did granddad feel cheated out of his inheritance? Had he kept the will as proof he was intended as the sole heir? Ah yes, but heir to what? After 'real estate' came that brief parenthesis '(if any)'.

Yes, but what about the other parenthesis: '(whose mother was Elizabeth Hewitt)'? Why the tense? Why specify? So she had died by the time he wrote the will. In a census form of that same year, great-granddad is described as a widower. So our granddad lost his mother before the age of ten. And was this the same Elizabeth named as the householder's wife in a census of 1881? Then, if so, what could 'natural' mean if not 'not adopted'? But perhaps my great-granddad had been passing her off as his wife while the census-taker sat there filling out a form.

The 1891 census has granddad living in a George Harrison's lodgings with no other family than his dad – the widower. Family tradition has him brought up by his sisters. But by then they'd gone too. Sometime before her man made his will, my great-grandmother must have died. He had lost his wife … or fancy woman, Elizabeth Hewitt, and then been left alone with his only son.

But who was she? Was she his wife or not? Did she have red hair? Or brown? Or was she fair? And had my granddad ever known his own mother?

This great-grandma, born in Mrs Gaskell's Cranford round about 1847, was somebody none of us knew anything about beyond these scraps and questions – even though her blood was still flowing through our veins.

There being nowt to inherit though, what did granddad feel cheated out of anyway? He called his third son, his second to survive, by the same name as his father. In the silence surrounding his origins, had he tried to sire a fictional legitimacy for himself and his seed? We were the only descendants of that Robinson still to be bearing the common family name.

Perhaps the three surviving sisters had made granddad feel different, feel tainted, not part of the family proper. Or perhaps an absence of mothering left him with an emptiness for which he tried to compensate by telling all those stories, by latching on to that scrap of paper as a token of his being the true, the thwarted heir.

24

Had granddad felt the stain – unbleached by nobility or wealth – the stain of illegitimacy? Had his father and Elizabeth Hewitt not gone through a ceremony in which each said 'I will'?

Then the will that made granddad an executor and sole heir was not drawn up, signed, and witnessed so as validly to do what it said it would do. It was only a draft will, neither more nor less liable to be making things happen than a poem.

And what had I inherited – a spur to the imagination, a beckoning to populate that silence with such stories, as if setting to rights a life fissured at its moment of conception? Whatever, I leave it to you.

Or would it have been better not to break this silence, not follow this strain of wild seed gusted on currents of town air from a late nineteenth-century Manchester?

Then, dad, your elbows on the table among breakfast clutter and letters, both hands cradling your chin, you're making, though late in the day, a sudden slow confession: you were like your father all along.

And again I can hear the sounds of frustration, exasperation, of your 'don't be stupid, Julie!'

Then, from the distant gaze and prompt tears of old age, there comes a glimpse of that little lad leaping across great weed-sown cracks in flags around your parents' yard, your dreaming possibilities.

To think of you too lost in stories, only to be saved for the greatest of them all, the one about the Way, the Truth, and Life....

Then with such ways of digging up the past, each life becomes
its own Ur, Troy or Thebes, and each of us our own archeologist.

I'm staring at an upstairs window into one more opposite,
over backyards with laburnum, washing lines, and every brick
picked out in its particulars, the friable stained wall making me
imagine.

Then I'm like him, dad, taking after you.

But who would have thought his death could provoke such con-
fusion? For it brought out their wills for inspection, revealing
the executor's name.

The signs had been there for some while when mum called
one early Friday morning in July. She told how he'd brought up
some blood and called out 'Julie!'

Then mum had gone and cleaned him up, helped him lie
back down on his pillow, and returned to the kitchen to phone
and finish chores.

29

We meanwhile dropped everything and readied our departure.
But before the car was fully loaded, the telephone rang again.
Mum had gone to see how he was doing, and found no sign of life.

He was lying there, as if asleep, under the front window's still
closed curtains, the sound of an early bus passing on the avenue,
birdsong, the distant barking of police dogs from their kennels
barely disrupting that new domestic silence, that almost perfect
peace.

30

Yes, the doctor had come and confirmed it: dad had gone peace-
fully at home as he'd wanted, in his ninety-second year.

And his last spoken word really had been – her name.

FROM THE LIFE

I wasn't born in Liverpool, but came to live in the city at the age of three. My father's first parish was St Andrew's, Litherland, and the family moved into the vicarage behind the church in the year of Suez. We were to be there for six years. Liverpool, in the twilight of its hey-day, is the place I came to self-consciousness. It was still a thriving seaport, still a semblance of the gateway to empire it had been. We arrived just in time to take trams into the centre; I rode the length of the Overhead Railway before it was pulled down, and went for a river cruise on the *Royal Iris* – or perhaps it was the *Daffodil*?

The terraces around Stanley Road in Bootle and Litherland were still interrupted in 1956 by bombed sites and pre-fabs. A bomb had exploded next to the church. There men would stand in tight huddles dropping coins on the cindery earth between them. What were they doing? Gambling?

There was a patch of waste ground behind our house. The upstairs landing airing cupboard was my grandstand seat while the men from Johnson's Dyeworks played football in their lunch hour – until the hooter sounded and they disappeared.

Among my father's parishioners were the Veizeys. They became friends of the family, courtesy aunt and uncle for the next twenty-odd years. Aunty Gladys was the talker of the pair. 'Go to Bootle with your bother!' she'd say, and 'I *want* never gets....'

My father's vocation took us away from Liverpool not long before the Beatles released 'I Wanna Hold Your Hand', and we spent the next five years in Wigan. My brother and I were called into our parents' bedroom and told that we'd be leaving St Andrew's. I didn't want to move. Why did we have to go to a place with holes in the ground called pits?

It was Aunty Glad, principally, who kept us in touch with the city during those years away. She would visit regularly to help my mother with her growing brood and the vast St Catherine's vicarage. Gladys also bought me my first record: 'Little Children' by Billy J. Kramer and the Dakotas. The choice is itself an example of her wit.

She also took us to see *A Hard Day's Night* when it first came out in 1964. The pride with which she did this must have conveyed to me something about what it meant to be a Liverpudlian. The city was a place to which I had become inseparably connected – yet without ever having the sense that it was somewhere I belonged.

During the spring of 1967 my father moved to his third and final parish: St Michael, Garston, in the south of the city. Once again, I didn't want to go. By then, puberty had occurred and brought with it the usual teen humiliations, a personal interest in pop song lyrics, and plenty to sublimate one way or another.

Regular bouts of tonsillitis had turned me into a reader in bed, though serious addiction to literary book-worming didn't begin until encouraged by the English masters at school. By chance, or good fortune, we were to study Joyce's *A Portrait* for A-level. Just as I could read myself into that book, so *Dubliners* could resemble the city I lived in, and Alan Hodgkinson, the head of English retiring that year, presented me with a copy of the newly published Penguin *Ulysses*.

Penny Lane ran along the back of the school playing fields. I passed 'the shelter in the middle of the roundabout' whenever I took the 86 bus into town. It must have been about this time that a poem was read on John Peel's radio music show, a poem called 'The Entry of Christ into Liverpool' by the Mersey beat poet and painter Adrian Henri. There was something of a vogue for poetry taking place. One of my friends brought Michael Horowitz's anthology *The Children of Albion* into class and made his own versions of the jokey haiku to be found there. Later,

Eliot's selection of Pound and a slim *Selected Poems* of Robert Lowell would challenge ideas about what could go into a poem. So, between the ages of fifteen and seventeen, writing poetry developed from a prank into an obsession.

I picked up from this reading and listening the conviction that art could be made out of what surrounded you, out of street names, 'blue suburban skies', and the details of people's lives. I had already written a now lost poem called 'From Long Lane to Russell Road' (both in the vicinity of Garston Park) before discovering Roy Fisher's *City*, Edwin Morgan's 'Glasgow Sonnets', or Charles Olson's *Maximus Poems* about Gloucester, Massachusetts, all encountered when reading English at York.

The spring 1974 issue of the York student magazine contains a curious 'stanzaic section from a long poem' which attempts to combine the 'church monument' style of George Herbert with the leading Black Mountaineer's poetry:

> St Michael's Parish Church is
> The third edifice
> And stands near,
> Since 1891, the gasworks
> And the dock railway tracks.
> It was here ...

And so it goes on, for thirty-odd more lines. Leaving Liverpool had meant encountering many different ways of seeing the relations between poetry and places. I would bring them all back home and try them out for size; though many, such as the above, would have to be discarded on the way.

'From Long Lane to Russell Road': but it wasn't only personal associations and alliteration that drew me to those places as a first serious subject for poems. My brother and I were dayboys at Liverpool College – on the half-fees arranged for the 'genteel poor' children of the Anglican clergy. This raises the inescapable question of class and, more generally, a growing awareness of divisions. Some of this awareness comes from the social position of the vicarage. To his children, a vicar appears to be invested with a mysterious importance by those whom he meets. Yet an Anglican clergyman's family is, simultaneously, in an ambiguous relation to this cultural aura. There was also the equivocal privilege of the large houses we would live in; these were places my parents could barely furnish and heat, but which nevertheless marked us out in my father's working-class parishes at the very moment we were supposed to belong.

At school the divisions were reversed: I became friends with the children of middle-class businessmen from Aigburth, Allerton, Woolton, and Harold Wilson's constituency, Huyton. These were more prosperous districts that surrounded the working-class, dockside village slum of Garston and, next door, the overspill estates of Speke. Sharp contrasts in wealth, social aspirations and possibilities were laid out as the pattern of avenues and districts in South Liverpool's semi-rural urban sprawl.

Growing up in Garston during the second half of the 1960s and first years of the next decade, I was not one of those who needed to be told by Asa Briggs in his *A Social History of England* that 'Liverpool went through an economic, social and political crisis'. My father's necessarily polite, but distant, relations with Free Masonry, the Orange Lodge, and the far Left, or my own first encounters with middle-class anti-Semitism and racial tension are some of the ways in which these crises were brought home.

The old Garston dockside area 'under the bridge' was to be demolished as a means to upgrade the housing stock. My father became involved in efforts to preserve the street communities of his parish against the wholesale dumping of populations in high-rise estates miles from anywhere they knew as home.

The fact that he had an aura, a status, a place in society which meant he could perform so useful a role in the city, set me thinking about the absence of such a position for the participant-observer poet, a stance for which his five changes of parish, as first curate then vicar, had peculiarly prepared me.

At this time, too, a verbal awareness of differences had insinuated itself. During the five years in Wigan I lost whatever Liverpool accent I'd picked up in the schoolyard of Linacre Infants, Bootle, and adopted the altogether different tones of the mid-Lancs coalfield. In south Liverpool where the middle class speaks a more refined Liverpudlian, my Wigan sounds were a cause of some skitting, and for the only time in my life I consciously adjusted my accent.

Almost twenty years later, I would have imagined that extended contact with the world of universities in other parts of Britain had reduced the Liverpool echoes to a neutral inaudibility, but not so. Debating whether the rhyme of 'gone' and 'one' is a full chime or an ironic dissonance (for me the vowel sounds are exactly the same), I found myself out-manoeuvred by having my accent characterized by a professor of very close reading as 'post-Beatles'.

Shaped by the city that went from pre-fabs to post-Beatles in my childhood and youth, I wouldn't want to deny it. In Japan people occasionally wanted to know what my hometown is, and despite the doubt about birthplace, or where the most years have been spent, I'd always answer: Liverpool.

This would immediately produce a mention of the Fab Four, and sometimes I was asked which is my favourite. When I selected poems of my own to include in *Liverpool Accents: Seven Poets and a City*, an anthology I edited in 1996, many of them were set in the city, and of the exceptions, 'For Different Friends' contains a concealed reference to one of their hits. It began as an elegy for the singer shot dead outside the Dakota Building in New York on 8 December 1980, and though the poem shed its original occasion, a trace of the starting point can be heard in the echo of lines from 'Help!' ('and I do appreciate you being round. / Help me get my feet back on the ground ...'). After the 'indisputable ground' of the first verse, there are the 'frozen solid marks / of bicycles, feet – familiar things' in the second, and

> Walking then among the trees'
> angular, elongated
> branches' shadows cast like arteries,
> I appreciated
> the pausing, unemphatic breath
> of another speaking.

Almost exactly a hundred years before John Lennon's death, Gerard Manley Hopkins complained in a letter to R. W. Dixon (22 December 1880) that 'Liverpool is of all places the most museless.' But it hasn't been like that for me.

The first thing that comes to mind of those years as a pupil at Linacre Infants and Junior School is smooth red brick and rough grey asphalt, the tall windows, and a big thermometer on a wall by the entrance. Presumably the thermometer was there so that we wouldn't play out if the temperature dropped too low. But if these details are confused or mistaken, it's because we moved around in my childhood and they have been lumped together with things from different places.

There were two playgrounds, divided by a wall. The one on the left, if you were facing towards the Mersey, was for the Infants; the larger one on the right, for the Juniors. The sports day events were held in the larger one. We sat on thin rubber mats as we waited to take part in the races. That's me sitting on one in the class photograph taken in front of the Infants School, a black and white class photo that lay around unconsidered in my parents' houses for years and years. I'm the little chubby boy in the middle on the front row. You can tell from the clothes we're wearing that it's summer. I've got on some Clarks sandals with creamy-white crape soles. It used to upset me when, after wearing them for a while, the soles wore thin and turned black. If you look closely, you can see that this has happened to mine.

On my immediate left in the photograph is Barbara Penny. On the other side from her is Colin Wells. On the back row, three from the left is Billy Morrison. When the school's centenary was announced in Liverpool, with a call for memories and memorabilia, Billy heard about it from his family, found me on the Internet, and sent a message from British Columbia, in which he added some more names to the faces. On the third row, second from the left, is Paul Thompson, who when last heard of was in Australia. Leslie Beattie is just behind me and she may still live in Bootle. Philip Stopford, back row, centre, is somewhere in Ontario. There is also a Billy Smith in the picture. He died a few years ago. Next to me on the other side is Sally McLeod. The girl on the back row nearest to the right is called Carol, I think. The boy with dark wavy hair in the centre of the middle row may be Glyn Hughes. There was also an Indian boy in our class at some point, though he must have arrived later. I can't exactly date the photograph, but perhaps it's from our first year – the late spring or summer of 1959.

There was a sand tray in the first-year classroom. It wasn't very big, and I can vaguely recall standing about in that room, or moving from one place to another, new to school life, not really understanding what I was supposed to be doing there. We sat around communal tables with maybe four children at each one for the lessons. There were also the usual big cards stuck high up on the walls, with 'A is for apple' and a picture of an apple – and so on. That's where we began to read, and I can still recall the *Janet and John* books. The teaching of reading was pretty successful in my case, because before leaving the school in 1962 I was borrowing big hardback books about fighter pilots and other war heroes from the local public library.

School must have started for me in September 1958, at 5 years and 8 months. I have a vividly painful memory of my first day at school. We are out in the playground, so it must be playtime, and it seems to be the morning. I'm standing around on my own, and that's because I don't know anyone yet. Up near the wall of the school is a small area fenced round with wooden sticks that are wired together. Because the playground has a hard floor, the fence doesn't stand up well, and has partly collapsed. Inside the fence there are some metal children's toys – a kind of rocking horse thing among them. Having nothing else to do, I climb over the fence and start to play on them. No sooner have I done this, than a teacher comes over and tells me to get out of there. Those are for the kindergarten children. So off I get, and go back to the schoolyard – feeling very ashamed of myself. Most of my strongest memories of these years are connected with being scolded, though I don't believe myself to have been a naughty boy.

In the second-year class I didn't like the teacher so much. Yet this is likely to be only because we had a confrontation about reading. What Miss – I can't recall her name – used to do was to set us all to work on something. It comes back to me as I write that we learned how to tell the time in this class. Then she would call us up to her desk, one by one, and we would read things out loud to her. At the back of one reading book were some word lists, written in very small print. As I was reading these out, she stopped me and corrected one of the words. But I kept insisting that what I had read was right – until finally she told me to look at it again more carefully. And I realized that I had been wrong. So there we are again: more feelings of shame, and another clear memory among the general blur.

The third class comes back as the one with the warmest glow. Maybe I had become the teacher's pet without knowing it. My only clear memories of this year also involve things that were to become among the most important in my life. I have a sharp sensation of puzzlement concerning a joke that involved play on words. It was something like 'Why did the cow slip?' 'Because it wanted....' But I can't remember the punch line. It was a pun on the name of the flower: a 'cowslip'. I didn't get it – but I did realize something was going on that I needed to understand.

The other memory is of doing a still-life drawing with col-oured pencils of an apple, and taking special care over the different colours of peel around where the core came out. I think the teacher must have complimented me on this, otherwise why would I remember it? Is it possible that we used to write with pieces of chalk on little blackboards with a wooden frame around them? Is that how we practised our letters? I have a memory of ink wells in the desk with turquoise ink and dipping pens that used to get clogged and make nasty blots – but this must be from the Junior School, or even later at my next school.

The other thing we did that comes back clearly is 'Music and Movement'. This we did in a little gym. The music came from a radio. So there must have been some special programmes broadcast just for schools. The voice on the radio would tell you to pretend to be a tree, and there would be some tree-like music while you did it. Then the voice would say that a strong wind has started blowing and all the little trees will have been told to sway their branches – which we did to the special effects sounds. We also used to do dancing in this class. This certainly involved having partners, and I can recall that there was a certain amount of negotiating about who would dance with whom. Yes, we had our little favourites. So, now, looking at the class photograph, I can almost bring back some of the things that we said to each other. I certainly quarrelled with Colin Wells at one point, and I can remember saying something rather cruel to Barbara Penny as well – but this happened out of school.

If I did start at Linacre in September 1958, then we went up to junior school in autumn of 1961. I can only have done one year at the most, because my dad moved to St Catherine's, Wigan, sometime in 1962. In junior school the lessons got harder, of course. I can recall us sitting in rows of desks that were raised on shallow steps towards the back of the class. There we all are reciting our times-tables out loud. One two's two, two two's are four ... twelve twelves are a hundred and forty-four.

Learning to write also got much more serious, because I can recall clearly noticing that it was very easy to make the mistake of writing 'baddy' instead of 'daddy'. We may have also learned how to sew and weave in this class. This is where I wove a rainbow tea cosy that we still use. There was certainly some teaching of Greek myths, about which I remain fairly perplexed. I also remember realizing that there was something wrong with all the drawings we did of some grass, with a house on top of it, and over the roof a sun with lines coming out for the rays, then a stripe of blue for the sky. After all, if you look at it, the sky touches the roofs of the houses. The business about who was my 'girlfriend' in the class also seems to have got slightly more fraught at this time.

Ray Charles' song 'Hit the Road, Jack' – I discover from the Internet – was a US number one and a UK number six hit in 1961. I can recall clearly standing on the asphalt of the playground of the Junior School at about home time thinking that it would certainly hurt if you hit the road, and wondering why Jack would want to do it anyway.

In those days we were never collected from school. My parents certainly warned me not to talk to strangers, and never take any short cuts down back entries. Nothing frightening ever happened, mind you; and I don't actually recall any particularly violent experiences in the playground either. The only time I got hurt in the street was when I walked straight into a lamppost. There don't seem to have been any serious bullies. This was to change in Wigan, where the parish was poorer and the kids more violent. But maybe it was because we boys were getting older.

'Hit the road, Jack, and don't you come back no more, no more.' Perhaps the reason I remember thinking my painfully literal thoughts about the words of Ray Charles's song is that I was about to hit the road myself. Certainly, since leaving Linacre in 1962, I haven't met or spoken to any of the people in the photograph again.

Somewhere there's a family photograph taken on a beach that
may be at South Shields. My mother is sitting in the opening of
a pup tent, looking after my baby sister. My brother has dug a
deep hole in the sand and continues to work on it nearby. I'm in
the hole, reading a book. Though I can't be sure what the book
in the holiday snap is, something tells me it's a large hardback
borrowed from the local public library on Ocean Road. It is, or
it might as well be, a history of the aeroplanes built before and
during the First World War by Fokkers – one packed with barely
comprehensible technical specifications for engines or guns,
about how they invented the synchronizing gear which let them
fire through the propellor without shooting themselves down.
Why am I reading such a book? Why am I reading it with so
much concentration as if oblivious to being there on the beach?
This photo presents me with two problems: how did I come to
be in that hole, and how would I get out of it?

The earliest book I remember reading, or being helped to
read, was the tale of the hen afraid that the sky would fall. I
know she thinks it actually has, but she's mistaken, isn't she?
Even at infants school I may have been something of a critical
reader, for I recall that the story puzzled me. If you looked up,
you could see that the sky didn't stop; it just went on and on.
I'm a vicarage child who grew up where the words 'heaven' and
'the heavens' had assumed references. The sky wasn't like a lid
or a ceiling, was it? So how could you think it might fall down?
And if it couldn't, then what had the poor hen been afraid of
anyway? The wrong thing, I assume, if her and her friends' fate
at the hands of the fox is the moral of the story.

My identity, it now seems, emerged from such puzzles about
looking up and finding meaning. My mother's parents' house by
the North Sea at the mouth of the Tyne was where we regularly

spent holidays – such as the one that may have produced that photo of us on the beach. From the roof of the nave in a church we used to attend, a wooden model ship had been suspended. Gazing up at this beautifully crafted boat, I heard the congregation singing 'O worship the Lord all glorious above' and mistook the verb for 'warship'. My parents were much amused when I asked them what 'warship the Lord' meant.

But, then, wars and rumours of war were all around. Being born in 1953, a Coronation baby, meant also being born in the last year of the Korean War, when wartime rationing finally ended, less than a decade after the atom bombs and the Japanese surrender. My father was thirty-three when he first became a parent, and my mother twenty-six. They had met at Durham University in about 1947 and were starting a family slightly late for people of their class and times – about six years late. My mother's father had been wounded at Gallipoli in 1915 and, as a very small boy, I was told about the pieces of shrapnel still lodged somewhere inside him. But it wasn't only the wars in which members of the family fought that fuelled my reading habits.

In Liverpool around 1961 there was an exhibition at the City Museum commemorating the outbreak of the American Civil War a century before. My parents took us and that started a bout of devouring books about Stonewall Jackson and Robert E. Lee. Liverpool had sided, at least covertly, with the Confederacy. The *Alabama*, a blockade-runner, was built in Birkenhead. While not understanding anything about the Lancashire cotton industry and its links to the slave plantations, I caught this leaning towards the South – because the imagined heroics of the soldiers with grey uniforms were far more fatefully intriguing. Perhaps this temperamental habit of siding with the bound-to-lose stems from, or is at least illustrated by, that obsession – as by a somewhat later addiction to books on the American Indian Wars. It's a habit that must have been strengthened through being taught history from the Civil War to Bonnie Prince Charlie by a Catholic master at Wigan Grammar School.

Doubtless, there were innumerable boys my age who played with toy guns and refought the battles of parents' and grandparents' youths, but not all of them will have been inclined to plough through biographies and military histories to feed the imagination with pictures of what it may actually have been like. Two things probably encouraged the growth of this insatiable reading. My father moved from one parish to another when I was three, nine, and fourteen: that landed me in suddenly friendless phases at crucial moments. Then there were the regular bouts of tonsillitis and other childhood illnesses that were got through by going to bed with books.

A memory comes back from our Wigan years: I'm reading a series of flying doctor stories – aeroplanes again – which were set in Africa and involved missionary work. These must have been consumed during a fervently religious phase from about eight to twelve, during which I seriously contemplated following my father into the Ministry. I was a choir boy and, of course, a regular church attender. My introduction to English poetry came through *Hymns Ancient & Modern*: 'As o'er each continent and island / Dawn leads on to another day'; 'In the bleak midwinter / Frosty winds made moan. / Earth stood hard as iron, / Water like a stone.' I'm quoting from memory. The repeated singing of songs is still something I do, whether under my breath or aloud. A musician friend recently described me as a walking songbook.

Another memory comes back sharp and clear: I'm standing on the front row of the congregation in a church that isn't my father's. We're all singing 'Jerusalem' – a song beginning intriguingly with a conjunction: 'And did those feet....' Of course, I didn't know who wrote it, but the words seemed terribly relevant: 'those dark Satanic mills'. As far as I'm concerned they're cotton mills. 'Bring me my arrows of desire', we sang. This is the memory: though I'm singing too, my eyes are fixed on the legs of a girl standing out in front with a group of others all wearing their Sunday best. One leg is bent at the knee and the heel slightly lifted. I'm fascinated by 'those feet', become conscious of looking, and think I shouldn't, but don't want to stop. So that earliest awareness of my being attracted to girls is inextricably entangled with those words by William Blake.

The first poem I was conscious of hearing being quoted was John Masefield's 'Cargoes'. Nobody required me to learn it off by heart, as Paul Muldoon was – if that detail in his poem 'Profumo' is autobiographical. No, it was my father who'd memorized it at school. On the wall above the dining table in his mother's house at 472 Claremont Road, Rusholme, was a painting of an old cargo boat called the ss *Hardanger*. I was obsessed with it and, as if to supply a text, once dad reconstructed Masefield's third verse for us:

> Dirty British coaster with a salt-caked smoke stack
> Butting through the Channel in the mad March days,
> With a cargo of Tyne coal,
> Road-rail, pig-lead,
> Firewood, iron-ware, and cheap tin trays.

Many years later, when it will have come as a God-send, I would discover in his study a book called *The Modern Poet: An Anthology*, edited by someone called Gwendolen Murphy and published by Sidgwick & Jackson in May 1938. It's a well-informed, up-to-date volume with samples of work by Georgians, Modernists, the Auden group, and other new poets of the same decade, both famous and not so – from Robert Graves and Laura Riding to David Gascoyne, Kathleen J. Raine, Charles Madge, and even the Liverpool poet A. S. J. Tessimond. This book contains the inscription 'My Best Friend, / from / Lawrie / Christmas 1938'. Lawrie McAlpine was the vicar's son at Holy Trinity, Platt, in Manchester. Though a pacifist, he joined the Royal Engineers, convincing himself that peace would have to be fought for. He was crushed in 1944 when something fell off a transporter in Normandy.

The transition in reading habits from war to love took place, naturally enough, during teenage. I had a copy of a Biggles book set during the First World War where our hero is serving with the RFC on the Western Front. In it, there was a semi-romantic chapter where Biggles becomes involved with a Mata Hari enemy spy who he has reluctantly to leave when he discovers the truth. That story by W. E. Johns helped to fuel a good deal of vague sexual fantasy. The obsession with technicalities of early aeroplanes was about to metamorphose into a passion for other sorts of minute detail. So here you have me about thirteen, mainly interested in history and art, reading technical books about aeroplanes I can't fully understand, sliding from an obsession with war alone, to war and love, yet someone who doesn't have any real interest in literature. But I was volunteering to act in the annual school play.

At about this time I got the part of Denis, the bad-boy lead in a combined production with the local Girls High School of a musical about children being evacuated from London during the Blitz. Later parts included the White Rabbit in *Alice in Wonderland*, and Doctor Livesey in *Treasure Island*. But the highlight of all this was the musical – the occasion for my first 'relationships' at an age I now think woefully young. That I can still remember the names of the girls with whom I was involved, however briefly and superficially, suggests that they were coming to play a role in my imaginative life that would have astonished them had they known. While involved with the play about the Blitz and with Susan Fleming, the female lead, who happened to be our woodwork teacher's daughter, I came bottom of the class in English.

Literature began for me when we moved back to the Mersey in the spring of 1967, where I was lucky to come into contact with two devoted English teachers, Peter Stott and Alan Hodgkinson. It was they who first noticed, then encouraged, the reader and writer. They made me the library prefect in the sixth form, which must have been the year I bought a *Selected Poems of William Blake* ed. F. W. Bateson – on the day the currency went decimal in 1971. This fact is noted in the front where my name is also scribbled with its three initials. Preserved in the book is part of the half-title page to Trevor Huddleston's *Naught for your Comfort*, about his experiences of Apartheid, on the back of which is written in my best hand:

from *The Book of Thel.*

Why cannot the ear be closed to its own destruction?
Or the glist'ning eye to the poison of a smile?
Why are the eyelids stored with arrows ready drawn,
Where a thousand fighting men in ambush lie?
Or an Eye of gifts & graces showring fruits & coined gold?
Why a tongue impressed with honey from every wind?
Why an ear, a whirlpool fierce to draw creations in?
Why a nostril wide inhaling terror, trembling and affright?
Why a tender curb upon the youthful burning boy?
Why a little curtain of flesh on the bed of our desire?

Bateson's selection includes nothing from the Prophetic Books. I'll have found this in the school library, and copied it down when on duty during a lunch break. My having done this, with a heavy symbolism on the back of that title page, suggests a partial emergence from the hole on the beach.

The first piece of writing I took at all seriously was a project set by Mr Stott where we had to find something in a newspaper and write a summary. I produced a detailed account of the Six Day War from 5–10 June 1967. Mr Stott was complimentary about it, but with a tone of surprise. He may have been unprepared because I was simply hopeless at reading out loud in class. The occasions when it was my turn were agony. I couldn't pitch the phrases so that they sounded like sentences. My eyes would focus on one word at a time and I would be unable to pronounce it at all. The class just had to move on to the next boy, leaving me baffled and ashamed. How could someone who took such interest in books be so inept at reading them aloud? And how did this person once bottom in English, who couldn't sight-read to save his life, turn into a person who three or four times a year stands up in public to recite his own words, who reads texts to his students every week, who teaches the intonation patterns of English to second-language learners, and does Harry Potter for his children on a nightly basis?

Perhaps the explanation is that my difficulty with hearing and reproducing the cadences of English was what introduced me to its complexities, to the ways in which words and phrases can mean quite different things if said in ever so slightly altered ways. Whatever the explanation, fluency and assurance about the sounds of words has never been my hallmark. Not being able to foresee the pitch contours of sentences meant reading the words one by one, without projecting onto them a presupposed sense of the sentence's meaning. That's perhaps a useful thing for a poet, because you avoid the pre-formed and presumed. Everything has to be found as if from scratch with the individual words forming the meaning-structures. Not being adept at reading aloud may have meant not being too preconditioned to the sounds that English sentences were supposed to make. Even as a graduate student at Cambridge, I recall one contemporary expressing surprise that I read poems with such unexpected implications, but it was also he who noticed that some lines of mine asked to be intonated in two distinct ways to mean relevantly different things.

So it looks like my difficulty with reading was what kept me at it, what pushed me towards being this kind of reader and writer. Fiction has also proved a problem. The difficulty is that

I'm conscious of a permanent commentary going on in my head as I'm reading. It can be critical, but it may also be simply associative. So there I am, reading novels for English homework, or for term-time essays, or later so as to teach them, or for pleasure even, and I'll get to the bottom of the page only to realize nothing of the plot has stuck. Don't get me wrong: I went though all James Joyce (aside from *Finnegans Wake*) about this time, and can recall soaking my way through *The Waves* in the bath. Just as I read poetry against the grain of my sensibility and taste, so I manage a fair number of novels a year.

Yet they probably take me longer than for real addicts who give themselves up to them. I have to keep stopping to think or dream, then go back to pick up the thread of the story. The fact that lyric poems have relatively few words and have all those technical devices to focus interpretive attention may be why I manage with them better. It may also be that poems often invite an associative reading – or that you can learn how they're meant to sound, so they are halfway to being songs. Since they're so much shorter, you can readily experience their formal wholeness, while that of novels must be constructed over time in memory.

Often in poems it's not just a matter of reading the words either. As with jokes, you have to 'get' them. For similar reasons, I'm fond of reading aphorisms and books of philosophy that are written in short sections – Lichtenberg's pennyworths of truth or Wittgenstein's *Tractatus*. With the latter, it goes without saying, my first reading had me fairly baffled. Yet, again, those years of ploughing through technical histories may have borne fruit. It's perhaps not such a large stride, after all, from a book on early aeroplanes to the work of a philosopher whose oeuvre includes a patent for 'Improvements in Propellers Applicable for Aerial Machines' drawn up in Manchester during Wittgenstein's studies there, a patent accepted on 17 August 1911.

My final move from obsession with war to engagement in art came at the end of the first term at York University, when I arranged to transfer from the joint English and History degree to one in English only. R. T. Jones asked in the brief interview why I wanted to change course. Whatever my answer, I won't have said that already writing, and meaning to write more, I would have to read both intensively and extensively. There was a French Symbolists paper being offered by my tutor, Nicole Ward Jouve, and I wanted and needed to take it. My grasp of languages was, and still is, by no means secure. Here's another case of an attraction to the experience of deciphering something that you don't wholly grasp. So what does all this go to prove? I've recently come across a reference to 'that endangered species, the general reader.' Yet who is this? We all have a story behind why we read or what we choose to read. And when it comes to readers, I've always preferred the particular to the general.

A Performing Art

Were you to ask a poet if poetry is a performing art, you might discover from the answer much about the kind of poet to whom you were talking. For some poets, whose poems are made of sounds but not words, their work exists solely to be performed; others, whose poems are visual arrangements of letters or words in attractive images, justly aspire to the silence of a gallery. Performance gives rhythmic life to the sometimes cleverly arresting lyrics of pop songs, and there are poets who have tried to emulate the enthusiasm and appeal of pop concerts. For poets who do not make sound poems or concrete poems, are not would-be pop stars or performance artists, the question may be harder to answer. Speaking is inherently ambiguous, often requiring interpolation or gesture to make the meaning clear, and when you read a text out loud close attention is needed from the listener to distinguish, for example, 'torque' from 'talk' by the context, or 'where, as' from 'whereas' by the stress and intonation. In a publicity statement for one concert of readings the organizers said that they aimed to bring the lyre back into poetry. Without a text to which listeners might refer, their statement could well be mistaken for a rephrasing of the old doctrine that poets are liars and should be excluded from the city.

Why go and listen to poets reading their own work if the meanings may be obscure without looking at a copy of the printed words? Critics have drawn attention to the literary significance of Keats's physical stature, T. S. Eliot's dental record, Byron's deformed foot, or his dieting.... A corpus of work is created by a particular body, and in the first place I'd go to see a poet read as much as, if not more than, to listen. This was one of the premises of the Cambridge International Poetry Festival, which was held every two years between 1975 and 1985. I can still quite clearly picture Hans Magnus

Enzensberger at the third festival in June 1979 on stage in the darkened Corn Exchange at Cambridge. He was reading from his poem *The Sinking of the Titanic* in German and his own English translation. Enzensberger's face was extremely mobile: ingenuousness, sarcasm, disgust and pity passed across his features as he read. He had been in Italy and was wearing a white summer suit that seemed slightly luminous under the spotlights. When he reached the end of the poem where imaginary and symbolic passengers are swimming away from the ship, Enzensberger seemed to have turned the darkness of the Corn Exchange into an Atlantic Ocean.

Just as it can be a pleasantly confusing surprise to see for the first time the face of a radio personality whose voice is a part of your domestic furniture, so too putting a physical presence and a vocal timbre to poems you've read aloud to yourself adds a new tone to their music. Poems and lines that have seemed shapeless or badly constructed may appear to have form in the poet's own mouth. It's for you to judge whether or not the poem's supposed form is an imaginary rhythm forced onto the words – a rhythm they do not inherently sustain. The same may be true of a poet who believes a poem to be awfully affecting and who therefore changes tone of voice to convey this as the poem's false climax approaches.

There will be productive conflict between the rhythm and intonation of a poem. This struggle of the stress pattern with the implied emphases exists as a variable equilibrium within good poems. At a memorial reading of work by Vittorio Sereni, who had died two months before he would have attended the 1983 Cambridge festival, these different aspects of his poetry were drawn out by the contrasting styles of his near contemporary Franco Fortini and the younger Maurizio Cucchi. Sacrificing some of Sereni's rhythmic continuity, Franco Fortini read expressively in a staccato – sharply emphasizing both syntactic stops and line-endings. The approach implied an interpretation of every detail, and was one of the most effective attempts I have heard to convey one meaning of a poem in a language foreign to most of the audience. By contrast, Cucchi read with little insistence in a quiet, melodic voice that finely conveyed the through-composed cadences of Sereni's lines and stanzas.

The ancillary art of poetry translation was tried in performance at each Cambridge Poetry Festival starting with the founder Richard Burns' in 1975. Listening to readings of poetry in other languages followed by English versions, you are confronted with both the untranslatable and the translated. The applause that greets a poem in another language passionately delivered by its writer may sometimes be little more than well-meaning homage to a principle, but much is to be gained from paying attention to the sound of other poetries and glimpsing different assumptions about its power in the unfamiliar modes of reading, little from defensively imagining that ours is the only possible situation. Nor is it satisfactory to argue that because poetry cannot be fully translated you should not bother with partial achievements. It is important to reflect at intervals upon the position in the world of your own country and culture, and an instructive place to do this is in an international poetry reading where such contrasting outlooks are implicitly and sometimes directly aired.

Both the English language and its poetry in Britain are incalculably indebted to influxions of linguistic influence from abroad; the quality of British poetry now and to come will depend upon the character of the country's life and culture, yet also upon an openness to the importance of developments elsewhere. Translators engaged upon the inherently vulnerable task of bringing something of their original over into English will experience divided loyalties to the art of the other and that of their own language; they are nevertheless an indispensable part of a poetry festival and a living literature. Because the translators have the advantage of an audience that can more readily understand the language of their piece, they had better not exploit that familiarity to up-stage, and further distance, the more intractable original. Rosemarie Waldrop's renderings of work by Edmond Jabès at the Cambridge festival in 1979 are an exemplary instance for me, and in 1981 you could compare, after Josef Brodsky had read poems by Osip Mandelstam, a bevy of translators' attempts to convey, honour, rival and even possess the great Russian poet's texts.

Much can be deduced about poets' relations to themselves, their poetry and its public by what they say to the audience between poems. Some poets over-prepare the event; they not only know what pages they will read, but exactly how they will introduce each piece. Often they feel bound or tempted to explain what the poem is about: it is certainly more disappointing when they appear correct than when they seem wrong. Sometimes the audience hears an anecdote about how the piece came to be written, or is given a brief tour of the formative events in the growth of the poet's mind. At others they will be informed of the writer's political tendency or literary allegiances. Then there are the pieces of indispensable information required to catch the next poem's drift, or acknowledgements of homage and indebtedness. Judging the ratio of talk to poetry may imply tact in the writer as a person, though not necessarily as an artist. Some poets have humorous stories that they intersperse with readings, or bits of lightly ironic crowd control. Roy Fisher dedicated a poem to his Cambridge audience in 1977 by saying something like: 'This is also for you as you've been so good ... so far.'

Though poets sometimes under-prepare or seem not to have prepared at all, it need not follow that their reading will be a disaster. Certainly in the attacks of nerves that poets undergo during performances they are capable of forgetting where the next poem they'd thought of reading comes in their own collected poems. The more traditionally bohemian, under the influence of excessive socializing, have been known to lapse into embarrassing anecdotage – yet I can only recall two or three such calamities in a decade of festivals. When W. S. Graham read at Heffers bookshop one lunch time in 1981, he appeared neither well nor well prepared. In the lengthy silences and mumblings between and sometimes within poems you wondered if he would be able to continue at all. His wife was close at hand encouraging him and mentioning titles of pieces he might read. Yet perhaps there was an element of play-acting in his performance, of putting on the helpless and difficult man: his late and oddly scatty elegies to painters or the poem addressed to his sleeping wife were very well served by precarious delivery, remotely resonant and secure within their author's apparent self-confusion.

In Cambridge, hearing a poem that I liked the sound of would probably lead me to the Festival bookstall; for the composed work has an ambivalent existence which seems satisfied neither by its utterance nor indeed its text alone. Between text and utterance too the combinations of emphasis are extensive. You might learn something of what your poet thinks or assumes about these two states from the word used to describe the action of turning a poem from an arrangement of print into one of air. Some poets rant, others declaim, some intone, others speak; they recite, or read, and some just say the poem. These varieties of delivery involve, as I have implied, different compromises between the meaning introduced into a sentence by the way in which it is spoken and the meaning a sentence introduces into a voice by the way it is written. Ezra Pound was drawing attention to the latter when he wrote a postcard to Mary Barnard on 23 February 1934:

Thing is to cut a shape in time. Sounds that stop the flow, and durations either of syllables, or implied between them, 'forced onto the voice' of the reader by nature of the 'verse'.

I think this is the right emphasis for a poet to bear in mind when composing, but what would it do to the reading style?

And is 'forced onto the voice' an accurate account of the relation between speech and writing when the poet reads?

You sometimes hear it said that a certain poet doesn't know how to read his or her own work. This may be a fair description of the situation, but it might also suggest that the concern has been primarily to write and that the poet believes the poem's character is in its cadences, its form, its syntax and diction – not in the emphases of particular words and dramatic intonation added by a performing and overtly interpreting voice. The poet may seem to be reading in an uncertain tone because a voice filled with the conscious awareness of what the speaker understands the piece to mean takes pre-emptive possession of both the poem and its auditors.

When a dramatist writes a part with a particular actress in mind he is shaping her speeches with the imagined sound of her speech shaping his. Staging a drama requires the directorial introduction of interpretive layers that can evidently make or mar what the dramatist wrote. But if you say that a poet didn't read his or her poem very well, you may also be implying that this doesn't matter: the business of making or marring has already taken place elsewhere before the poet steps onto the stage. A poem may be enhanced, but not realised from the podium. I don't much enjoy hearing actors performing poems because, excepting the most subtle and subdued, they so often seem to be attempting artificial respiration on a body which was already breathing without their assistance.

Soundless private reading is a solitary occupation. Within such isolation readers are free to gain pleasure and instruction according to the dictates of their own self-accompanying thoughts. You can always put the book down. At a poetry reading the listener is rather less at liberty. It's true that people sometimes leave ostentatiously to show their preferences or imply criticism. Yet occasionally even a favourite poet will read a piece you do not like and you are obliged to sit through it –

whereas in the powerful privacy of silent reading you might flick over a few pages or throw the thing aside.

Though this social obligation to endure parts of a reading may seem a drawback of poetry in performance, it does instance the direct nature of the relationship between audience and writer, a relation normally concealed behind the processes of publication, bookselling, reviewing and reading. It is useful occasionally for both poets and readers to have the opportunity of acknowledging each other's existences. In any decent relationship there will be moments to endure as well as those you enjoy. A poetry festival is a place where the poets and the readers come face to face with the evident yet occluded fact that, though made in separated privacy, culture is produced by and for a community. Like the society of which it is a part, the poetry community is at odds with itself. Its strengths and weaknesses are inextricably intertwined. Fellow feeling and friendship jostle with envious rivalry; wounded amour-propre is trying to take its revenge while colleagues are honouring each other's labours. The atmosphere itself is vital.

The ability to listen to others with imagination and understanding is a rarer quality than people think. The very best poets are more likely to be good listeners than impressive talkers. Perhaps sometimes poets write because they find it hard to speak, or find silence intimidating. There are poets whose work seems an invitation to experience vicariously the outpourings of words that went into the self-expression their poems display. I prefer to imagine that good poetry encourages constructive listening. The moment of inspiration for some poets, or, more accurately, what distracts them into the thought of a poem, comes with the impinging of an unforeseen noise: a door slamming, an out-board motor, English heard in another country, a car backfiring, a cuckoo clock…. And the process of composition can be an attending to the silence within your head from which the words slowly or suddenly emerge in mutual associations of sound and sense.

Listening to poetry being read may be an example of a Wordsworthian wise passiveness. You sit still, open to influences, actively engaged. The degrees of concentration required vary from poem to poem, poet to poet. Attention spans are short, but can be trained to let us hear more, more thoughtfully. Like awkward moments between acquaintances when you rack your brain for words to ease the tension, the mute instant between a poet's uttering a work's title and the first line is a vacuum that draws you into it. By the end, the poet reading to you will have tried to transform that emptiness into a hush replete with the senses of words – like the intimate quiet of friends where speech is no longer necessary. The poem will have succeeded if you hear, within the silence after its final line, a great relief in the feeling that now at last nothing further needs to be said.

In a Tight Corner

The social sciences library of Bradford University was, in the early 1970s, and may still be, above a skating rink. The muffled sounds of that decade's dance music would seep up to the few students at work on a Saturday morning, insidiously whispering that fun was to be had elsewhere. Though not attached to the university, I used to accompany my girlfriend there and take advantage of its contemporary poetry collection, the shelved slim volumes in mint condition. Among the many books that nobody wanted to read, I pulled out one with a sepia photograph of a pre-war street party on the jacket, noted the title and author, *Collected Poems 1968* by Roy Fisher, and decided to give it a try. I've never been able to ice skate.

In the early 1970s, the elders of Bradford, who would a few years later have David Hockney's *A Bigger Splash* banned from his home town's flea-pits, were arranging for its Victorian Gothic centre (attacked by Ruskin for aesthetic-moral hypocrisy) to be replaced by a then already dated style of cheapskate brutalism. Sitting in the social sciences library, reading for the first time works such as 'City', 'For Realism' and 'The Memorial Fountain', I had in my hands a key to begin understanding the processes which were substituting one grim environment for another in the town that I would visit with my own romantic notions every other weekend. Bradford could even boast a small estate of new box-like council houses, where, in a cold December 1974, I helped deliver the Christmas post, locally called – no, not 'Toyland', the title of an early poem by Fisher about Sunday in the suburbs, but 'Toytown'.

It's been suggested recently by another poet of about my age that Fisher's writings are important because they make us 'foreign to ourselves'. That is not how it felt to read him in a half-demolished Northern town just two years after *Collected Poems*

1968 had been published. I'd been introduced to a little modernist poetry ('Prufrock' and the 'Exile's Letter' from *Cathay*) in the sixth form, and followed up the lead in the school library by trying *The Waste Land* and 'Mauberley'. So even then it was possible to catch 'What are the roots that clutch, what branches grow / Out of this stony rubbish?' behind Fisher's line about Birmingham, 'What steps descend, what rails conduct?' And a not-so-distant relative of the woman who had asked: 'What are you thinking? What thinking? What?' could be heard wondering 'At least – why can't you have more walls?' in 'Experimenting'. 'What have you been reading, then?' asks the 'I' character in the same piece: modernist poems written by men of my grandfather's generation might have been one reply. Not only did Fisher's poetry indicate that there was a line linking me through a book published when I was sixteen to those famous works of about half a century before, it showed that such ways of writing could be directly relevant to the immediate environment. They seemed to be at work on the world where I had been born and grew.

Most of my 1970s was spent trying to teach myself how to write. The poems I published in little magazines and small press editions reveal the homage that is paid by indelible influence. Unlike the hapless student who, in one of Fisher's 'Paraphrases', writes to him exclaiming that 'It is / too late! for me to change / my subject to the work of a more / popular writer', I changed my doctoral dissertation topic to the work of three contemporary English poets, one of whom was the 'please Mr Fisher' of that burlesque. When I finally plucked up the courage to inform the poet of this fact (we had been in very occasional correspondence for a couple of years), he replied with a finely wrought minimalist postcard. The printed 'University of Keele, Department of American Studies', holding-note read 'Thank you very much for your letter concerning', but had been firmly cancelled with a black line, and the solitary word 'Judas!' inserted – a word whose initial shock effect was only slightly relieved by the '& best wishes, Roy.'

When crises come, they throw us back upon whatever reserves and resources we may have stored away – and so it was for me in the early years of the 1990s living in Japan where I couldn't really speak the language, going through the accelerating break-up of that same relationship (by then a marriage) which stretched back to Bradford's social sciences library, and on top of it all waiting to undergo major surgery for the removal of a brain tumour. The years spent compulsively reading Fisher's writings had left many echoes in the back of my head; so finally I let them act as a set of magnets for other words and phrases: 'A Well-Made Crisis', its title from the third of Fisher's 'Seven Attempted Moves', catches a moment of desolation outside the art department in Kyoto University where I was confronted by some dusty plaster casts of European sculpture; another poem, set back in England, travels down 'the old paths trouble knows' from his 'Diversions'; while the sequence 'A Burning Head' recalls one more question asked in 'Experimenting' ('Perhaps you've had a child secretly sometime?') with 'You'd got pregnant once and lost it? / How come I never knew?'

That same sequence describes being allowed home to convalesce about a week after the operation:

> Become a favourite of the night shift
> I hardly take up any time,
> am moved to ease bed shortages
> from ward to ward to visitors' room
> with apologies, repeated goodbyes: had left
> as if going home by gentle stages.

A glance at the earlier version of this sestet, published in *Stand*, reveals only too plainly its source: 'as if going home in easy stages' had been provided by another poem with a hospital connection. After the subsequent funeral in Fisher's 'As He Came Near Death', we mourners 'got out into our coloured cars and dispersed in easy stages.' It was one of those echoes that had slipped under my guard, but the shame-faced revision is no more than a fig leaf. 'Built for quoting in a tight corner – / *The power of dead imaginings to return*' is how the third of his 'Diversions' describes such haunting visitations by, for example, 'the ghost of a paper bag'. In his self-review, 'Roy Fisher on Roy Fisher', he describes himself as 'an effective phrase-maker, and he'd be eminently quotable, if only anybody could find a reason to quote him.' But it's been among my lots in life to find a host of them.

Japanese hospitals don't exactly have an appointments system.
If you think there's something wrong with you, you try to get
there as early as the admission opens, enter your name on a list
and then just wait for as long as it takes. It can take the best part
of a day. During 1992, living in Sendai, I began to hear a faint
tinnitus in my right ear and thought I was becoming slightly
deafer in that one than in the other. There's a poem made of four
fragments about this from *Lost & Found* (1997) called 'Hearing
Difficulties'. It begins:

> About the shell of my right ear
> it's true there's something ominous.
> Added to the chorus
>   of voices I can hear
> is a thin, continuous
> rushing noise like the sound of the sea
> or like an old valve record player
> left on through the night.

That autumn, while taking tablets for a supposed inner ear in-
fection, I started to feel stabbing pains across my right cheek, and,
unconvinced by the private clinic's diagnosis, booked myself in
to have some more extensive checks at the City Hospital – well,
not booked myself in, because I'm afraid my Japanese wasn't that
good; I'd been in the country for just over three years, and the
English department assistant had volunteered to act as a guide.

    Visiting professors in Japan can find themselves treated royally
by students and colleagues, and the social attitudes towards aca-
demics are far more respectful than in England. Such things can
go to your head, and on one occasion, waiting and waiting, I
complained to our assistant, Yasushi Saito, about the lack of a

more personal treatment. He quietly rebuked me. 'When it comes to sickness, we're all of us equal,' is what he said.

My first two years in the country had been spent in Kyoto, living in traditional-style houses, being taken to famous temples and beauty spots, suffering acute loneliness: my marriage was disintegrating, the time I spent alone being interrupted by brief and difficult visits from a wife whom I had known for over twenty years, but whom I was beginning not to recognize. The feeling may well have been mutual. This, however, is not the occasion to go into that story.

Japan being a place to learn patience, it must have been the third or fourth time we went through the hospital process that the specialist in the ENT department tentatively uttered the one word 'diagnosis' in English – and handed me a piece of paper with the words 'acoustic neuroma' on it. When I asked the assistant to ask him what it meant, the doctor again reached into his English vocabulary and found the words: 'brain tumour.' Out in the waiting area, among all the other people and their illnesses, I felt as if I'd been punched in the stomach:

> In a hearing clinic's waiting room
> someone's worse off than yourself;
> putting up the CT scan
> he shows what lies beneath the skin
> and bad news after hours of patience
> arrives in the shape
> of a paler shape about the size of a coin.

That half-line, 'what lies beneath the skin', remembers T. S. Eliot's phrase about Webster, who 'saw the skull beneath the skin' and 'was much possessed by death' – as indeed was I, sitting there among the other patients and digesting the simple words 'brain tumour': a diagnosis that (not knowing any better) I took to be tantamount to a death sentence.

In our head of department's office with the junior professor, Hiroshi Ozawa, and the assistant one day later, I found myself with a choice of having the tumour removed at the University Hospital in Sendai, or going back to England and undergoing the operation there. My decision to return home, where I could have family and friends nearby, was accepted with equanimity. So, at the ENT department in Addenbrookes, Cambridge, that early December, it was explained to me that mine was a benign tumour, and that, not being a cancer secondary, there was little chance of death (they had only lost one patient in some eighty operations) – though the side effects and the convalescence would be serious: partial deafness, some facial paralysis, headaches, chronic tiredness.... Since my tumour had been there for seven or eight years already, and was growing at a very slow rate, there was no danger in simply adding my name to the waiting list. They would let me know some time in January when the operation could be performed:

'God help you' comes from overseas.
It means the very best of luck
in the English of a Japanese,
and it's true you need it when

a consultant pats you on the knee
offering some courage,
lays his hands on you and says,
'You'll be wondering soon: why me?'

No sooner had I arrived in England than I began to receive 'Get Well' cards (and a tiny origami crane) from Japan – from Shoichiro Sakurai, for instance, the Kyoto professor who had first arranged for me to take up a one-year post there as a visiting lecturer. His knowledge of idiom is not perfect; but he evidently intended the phrase 'God help you' to be taken literally, which is how I took it.

However, it was not until some time in February that the hospital finally informed me that my operation was booked for 12 May 1993. Long before being told this, I reported the basic situation back to my department in Sendai by fax. Earlier in the new year, a reply had come from Japan which said that since I couldn't say when the operation was going to be, and could not fulfil my duties, my contract would be terminated at the end of March. This seemed the final blow: I was facing major surgery, my wife was divorcing me, and my job was lost as well. As the poem says, '... why me?'

> But I was thinking: Well, why not?
> What would they mean, the hours of boredom
> and jokes about a poet going deaf,
> all things being equal in sickness and in death,
> if not that here's just another of those people?
>
> So when you tell him we're getting a divorce
> (letting him know as a matter of course)
> he replies, 'It never rains but it pours.'

That's how 'Hearing Difficulties' ends, with no mention of the threatened job loss. Among the many reasons for its absence from this autobiographical collage is that only a day or two after getting the message terminating my contract, I received another which said something like: 'disregard previous fax'. What had happened?

From what I later gathered, it seems the head of department (a year or two away from retirement age) had gone to the dean and described my health predicament. Together, with the best interests of their faculty in mind, they had decided to replace me, so as to make sure that the visiting professorship post was not lost through falling vacant should I be unable to return by 31 March 1993 to re-sign the annual contract. The Ministry of Education had been making noises about abolishing such positions and its loss would mean a reduction in the faculty's standing in the Japanese academic world. It would mean the end of a tradition: the post I held had been occupied by, among others, Ralph Hodgson, George Barker and James Kirkup.

When he heard of this decision, the junior professor had telephoned the older Kyoto academic – in tears, as I was later told. During my first year in Japan, he had listened to a paper I gave on *The Rape of Lucrece* at a Shakespeare conference in Shikoku, and when, the following year, a vacancy in Sendai had arisen, he contacted me about the possibility that I might take up the position. He would also become the head of department in just a year or two and had expected that I would be his colleague during the interval when there might well be only himself and the foreign professor to run the English teaching. With or without the encouragement of my Kyoto sponsor, the junior professor confronted his senior and protested that terminating the contract in absentia was not the right course of action.

Such behaviour is (I understand) rather unusual in Japan; after all, a junior member of a hierarchy had opposed his direct senior in the faculty and, what's more, he had done it at least partly in the interests of a foreigner – someone categorically outside the hierarchy. At this point, the head of department, Zenzo Suzuki, also did an unusual thing: he suggested that, since there was a conflict between what he had done and what his junior felt should have been done, they would resolve the dilemma by asking the opinion of the only other member of the department on a salary from the Ministry of Education: the assistant, Yasushi, who had accompanied me on my hospital visits. He supported the younger man's point of view against his professor, the professor whose sponsorship would assist him in finding a post of his own while I was away. It was then that I received the second fax.

Once the decision had been reversed, the senior man put himself out to make sure that the new line of action would succeed. There followed complex bureaucratic processes for arranging that the post should be kept open over the course of one semester. A special intensive course was arranged with a visit by the foreign professor at the University of Tokyo, so half my credits could be granted to the students, the other half being covered by the department head's extra classes on Natsume Soseki. I would go off salary, but continue to rent my flat, and had to promise to be back in Japan again by 14 September 1993.

You don't just get up and walk away from brain surgery. The removal of the tumour required an eight-hour operation and a twenty-four hour anaesthetic. Modern hospital practice, however, puts the emphasis on rapid recovery by pushing patients to become autonomous again as soon as possible. I have a clear memory within a surrounding blur of coming to consciousness in the intensive care unit, finding myself attached to various machines with wires and tubes. The team, when they realized this, made a bold attempt to get me back on my feet. But the removal of the right inner ear had destroyed my ability to balance, and I immediately collapsed to the floor. The result of this total failure at the first hurdle was that I was moved out of intensive care, but into a separate room – where, among other things, I wouldn't scare the patients awaiting similar operations.

Just ten days after, having relearnt how to walk and other basic bodily skills, I was released into the community for convalescence – a process that was interrupted a month later when I suffered an infection of the right ear which produced newly unbearable headaches and was thought to be meningitis. Being back in hospital for two weeks of intravenous penicillin, and with the prospect of a second investigative operation to find out and put right whatever might be wrong, made me begin to doubt whether I would make that September deadline. However, by the end of August, and without need of a second operation, the ENT specialist at Addenbrookes felt confident enough of my improvement to allow me to take the twelve-hour flight to Japan. That autumn I was just about able to get through my classes, and kindly encouraged to cancel anything I felt unable to manage. Fortunately, the occasion didn't arise.

When I later spoke on the telephone to Sakurai, my Kyoto sponsor, who mentioned the junior professor's tears, he gave me a piece of advice. 'Don't,' he said, 'hold it against your head of department that he'd agreed to terminate your contract; it was nothing personal: he would have done the same with anyone in that situation.' Here was another lesson to learn.

However, reflecting over the years on what happened, I suspect the lessons may be more various and complex. After all, the junior professor and the assistant had not done the expected thing. If the older man, born in 1930, had behaved in what he thought were the best interests of the institution (regardless of the individual concerned), the younger, born in 1954, had done what he thought best (by following his own judgement and considering the individual). Nor, by trying not to take it personally, did I feel inclined to discount the kindness that had been shown me by the junior professor and the assistant, born in 1963 – a kindness which meant that within a year of returning to Japan I was able to become a father for the first time, and, within eighteen months (the no-fault divorce come through), was free to marry my first daughter's Italian mother. Being an unemployed semi-invalid would have made both of those events much less likely.

When I first went to Japan it was to take up a job. I didn't go there to develop a prior interest in the country, its language or arts. That I lived so long in Japan wasn't only because over the years I came to admire and enjoy qualities in the culture, qualities that helped me grow in unexpected ways, it was because at a crucial moment a few individuals particularly wanted me to be there. I am, and shall be, eternally grateful to them.

Behind 'Otterspool Prom'

Otterspool Prom

'O cursed spite'
Hamlet

There's a dazzle of sunlight on the low-tide river
and our far shore
has a silver-grey blur, bright as never, never,
ever before.

You see it's enough to bring tears to the eyes
by silhouetting trees,
winter boughs spidery on mist-like white skies
twitched in a breeze.

But then down the promenade its flyers release
their dragon-tailed kite;
frost on the pitches is shrinking by degrees;

a student's words return, her going 'England's shite!'
and I'm like 'Please
yourself' in sunshine born as if to set it right.

'Otterspool Prom' was first published in *The Times Literary Supplement* on 5 June 2008. I had not taught creative writing on a regular basis until I returned to England and came to work at the University of Reading, after my eighteen years in Japan. It's been intriguing and enlightening to lead weekly two-hour seminars in which students present their work, and have it discussed by their fellow writers. What has also been pleasantly surprising is the extent to which the group members, who if discussing a canonical author might have been fairly tongue-tied, would loquaciously engage in minutely constructive criticism of their contemporaries' writing, making points ranging from the adequacy of the punctuation to lacunae in plotting, character inconsistencies, and many other things that I hope they will go on to apply not only to their own writing, but also to the work of those canonical writers who had appeared to overawe them in literature seminars.

Most of the conversations have tended to be amicable and temperate, but occasionally there have been quite heated and vociferous exchanges. My poem 'Otterspool Prom' would not have come to be written without some words from the latter. One student's chosen project for the term was to write a collage prose piece based on gun crime in a Los Angeles high school. Most of the material for it had been discovered on the web, and then cast into an attempted imitation of Californian speech among armed minors in a poor district of the city. As chance would have it, there had happened to be, that term, a number of stories set in simulacra of American metropolitan areas; and in each case I had delicately raised the question of whether the handling of the spoken idiom was sufficiently convincing to carry the themes that were being explored. The bee in my bonnet at the time will have also contributed to what I was saying to the students, it being that the landscapes and societies of our own country are themselves a *terra incognita* under our very noses. It's not a new idea. George Borrow wrote in *Lavengro* (1851) that 'there are no countries in the world less known by the British than these selfsame British Islands'.

So I suggested to them, in the gentlest possible terms, that it helps when attempting creative composition, especially starting out, to write about something that you know, using experiences that have made strong impressions on you, and, most of all, that you can only make discoveries about the matter you want to write about if you attempt it in a language coming out of yourself.

That way the sounds and associations of words can interact in your mind to generate phrases and sentences, which, when you work on them and read them back to yourself may well illuminate what you are doing, may teach you things about yourself, and thus, whatever the outcome, the process, with luck, will have been a benefit anyway. So I suggested to the student of the Los Angeles high-school gun-crime story that she consider setting the work in one of the areas of Britain where, sadly, we also have teenage violence of an equivalent kind, even if not on an American scale. I will have mentioned a few such inner city areas, including parts of the place where I'd been raised – reminded of Liverpool by the shooting of the 11-year-old Rhys Jones in the car park of the Fir Tree pub in Croxteth on the evening of the 22 August 2007. I had imagined that my line of thought to the seminar group was practically a self-evident truth, but could sense some crowd feeling developing against the idea....

'I can't do that,' the student replied, 'England's shite!'

Well, her words did make me laugh, and out loud if I remember, given that I'd spent the last eighteen years on the other side of the planet, making the most of my economic migration, enjoying what I could in a country not my own, and wondering what the circumstances might have to be for my return. I lost the argument too: none of the students who were presenting works located in high-threat transatlantic environments relocated them in our own backstreets. And I would say, though it may sound mean, that in retrospect the student's sudden outburst seems the most creative bit of language use she came up with during the term. After all, her two-word phrase had identified the theme she should have been exploring in her work. What had made her reach the age of nineteen feeling that these words might be a true representation of the country in which she'd grown up, and, if they were, why? Her words got under my skin, if not on my nerves, interacting with snippets of usage and quotation filed away in the recesses of my mind.

Back at the beginning of the 1970s, I had been taken through *Hamlet* in minute detail for A-level. Not long after that creative writing seminar, my thoughts somehow drifted to Marcellus's 'Something is rotten in the state of Denmark'; to Hamlet being sent to England where it is 'no great matter' if he doesn't recover his wits because 'there the men are as mad as he' (as if Shakespeare added that plot twist just to work in the joke); and to Hamlet's couplet from Act 1: 'The time is out of joint: O cursed spite / That ever I was born to set it right!' The student's word 'shite' might have helped me recall the rhyme words, and I made up a short version of Hamlet's predicament: 'O cursed spite / Denmark's shite.'

A week or two after this incident we drove up to Liverpool for an overnight with my parents and, as is our habit, went out for a Sunday pub lunch on Otterspool promenade with its view across the river Mersey towards the Wirral side. It was a day of bright diffused misty sunlight in mid-February, a day briefly evoked as best as I can in 'Otterspool Prom', an improvised sonnet which was not planned as such before the writing process. I had jotted down words and phrases about some of the phenomena that moved me and made my eyes water, along with the odd accidental detail, like those people flying their Chinese-style kite.

English is not a language especially rich in rhymes. If the phrases I'm noting down seem to point towards a poem whose materials don't demand to be extended very far, and contain phrases with three rhyming echoes, then my mind will turn to the Petrarchan sonnet, a form requiring triple rhymes in its sestet. But the key thing that had to take place for the poem to happen was the association of that stirring scene beyond the pub window with the words of the creative writing student. Maybe the sudden plethora of rhymes helped that happen too. Not only is there the 'spite / kite / shite / right', but also the other sestet rhyme, foreshadowed in the second quatrain: 'trees / breeze / release / degrees / Please'.

Contributing to this association, there could have been the background of Rhys Jones's shooting, though I don't recall it consciously impinging on the writing process. I was certainly aware of the evident emotional contradictions in the student's words, and my relief at having finally returned home, where shame at your native land, unlikely to arise in expatriates' feelings about an elsewhere, is natural. Relief and shame: so the problems of being away and of being at home were combined for me in the implications of that student's colloquial phrase. Then what will have made me think there was something apt about imitating the youth-speak of 'I'm like' followed by the more long-in-the-tooth colloquialism, 'Please / yourself', must have been that it exemplifies the process of her words getting under my skin to the extent of sounding like her, and then performs an attempt to recover a dialect equilibrium of my own. Maybe the hook-line to Ricky Nelson's 'Garden Party' was also coming to my rescue: 'You see, you can't please everyone, so you got to please yourself.'

'No! I am not Prince Hamlet, nor was meant to be', as T. S. Eliot has it. Behind the arras of 'Otterspool Prom' there may, I fear, be a tired old Polonius advising the young, prompted by an ingrained temptation to try and take responsibility for the state of things; and yet, in the poem's concluding transfer of Hamlet's words from the Prince's duty to the sunshine that Sunday lunchtime, there may also be a recognition of limits to what can be amended, along with an implicitly expressed need for things still to come right, and not just for me in my return home, but more widely – as subliminally articulated in the closing rhymes of the intuited sonnet form. My hope is that in reading the poem, preferably aloud, you hear echoing within you the working out of those contradictory feelings and that analogy for a state of things being wrong, and of things still needing to be set right.

Lightning Source UK Ltd.
Milton Keynes UK
UKOW04f0815190615

253782UK00001B/22/P